MIXED EMOTIONS

Rachael Doherty

MINERVA PRESS
LONDON
ATLANTA MONTREUX SYDNEY

ISBN 1 86106 663 5

First Published 1997 by
MINERVA PRESS
195 Knightsbridge
London SW7 1RE

2nd Impression 1998

Printed in Great Britain for Minerva Press

MIXED EMOTIONS

For my grandad

Contents

The Somme

This field, beside which the river does flow,
Witnessed such carnage, decades ago.
Divided they fought, but blow by blow,
United they fell, both friend and foe.

'Your country needs you!' the poster had said,
Four words that thousands of volunteers read,
And so away to French soil they fled,
But most of them soon, alas, were dead.

Life wasn't easy for those who survived,
Each day in a trench they had to get by,
Living on tea and biscuits so dry,
Trying to keep morale on a high.

Infested with lice and racked with disease,
Spread by rats, themselves swamped with fleas,
Seeing the every day shiver and sneeze,
Sometimes in mud that came over the knees.

Then 'over the top' they prepared to fire,
Clambering over their own barbed wire,
Faced with a sight so grim and dire;
Bodies lay strewn in the bloody red mire.

Such wasted young lives were brought to a halt,
During that time of deadly assault,
People may argue just who was at fault,
But what of the dead in their earthy vault?

So here in this field, where their fate they did meet,
Their ghosts now march to a different beat,
Some may applaud their opposer's retreat,
But in death, all are as one in defeat.

Inside A Lonely Heart

Be still, I said
To the voices in my head
As they talked of such inconsequence
As I lay awake in bed.

Despondently I whined,
To the pictures in my mind
Whose startling reality
Was fiendishly unkind.

I counted my tears,
One each for all the years
I've struggled with the loneliness,
I've battled with the fears.

I need to start,
Before I fall apart,
The screams that echo round my body
Live inside a lonely heart.

Stray

She was there,
When we walked in the dogs' home,
A trembling skeletal wreck,
With unkempt feet on cold concrete,
And no name around her neck.

She was scared,
She'd lost all hope,
As she stared right back at me,
From behind those bars, her merciless scars
Displayed such cruelty.

Deep in thought I could read her mind,
She was saying "But don't you see?
There are dogs here galore,
Needing homes by the score,
All in better condition than me."

A chance was all she begged for,
So back home with me she came,
Her bruises were nursed, but importantly first,
Her trust I had to regain.

They say that time is a healer,
And that has proved to be true,
For the shadow-like stray, I rescued that day,
Has started her life, now, anew.

Today she is all I could wish for,
Such loyalty I've not seen before,
And now in this hound, I've undoubtedly found,
A loving friend for evermore.

Yesterday's Youth

In a field grow the poppies as crimson a red,
As that of the mountains of blood that was shed,
A sea of bright scarlet, a picture so still,
Overshadowed by a large wooden cross on a hill.
They grow in memoriam to those who're no more,
Who died in the random unfairness of war,
Their trenches remain, but the men are long gone.
Now we're over half a century on,
We look back on the days that were so many's last,
And see what lessons we can learn from the past,
To read the names of those that were killed,
And think of the unnecessary blood that was spilled,
A picture of a man, so gaunt like a ghost,
To hear the bugle play the mournful last post,
Are all timely reminders of the price of peace,
The moment when gunfire eventually ceased,
When normality meant nothing, it was but a word,
Through those years they had lived a life so absurd.
So when these red flowers grow year after year,
It will be said of the many men who died here,
They were gallant and brave and courageous you know,
But the majority were just an everyday hero,
From ordinary backgrounds, some wealthy, some poor,
United in battle, brought together by war,
For some a battle to merely survive,
While others less fortunate laid down their lives,
And when the news back home was received,

Countless people around the world grieved,
Widows and children who'd lost their loved ones,
Mothers and fathers who wept for their sons,
They'd fallen abruptly at the end of life's path,
Now their names are inscribed on each epitaph,
Along with those three words, "Lest we forget",
It's to them we owe the greatest of debts,
For these are the ones who will never grow old,
But through their comrades, their stories are told.
Yesterday's youth will laugh no more,
Left sleeping on a distant foreign shore,
Yesterday's youth, those willing young men;
When we talk of freedom, we owe it to them,
To remember how, and why they died,
So when you wear your poppy, wear it with pride.

My So-Called Friends

Whenever I need to reach out and touch
A helping hand when I'm hurting so much,
When I'm torn apart and bleeding inside,
I need a friend in which to confide.

I was once surrounded by people who cared,
Who listened whenever my soul was bared,
Who'd help whenever I felt confused,
But I was the one who was being used.

Popularity was always mine,
When I surrendered my spare time,
To taxi them from here to there,
To give them lifts and pay their fare.

But when the dirt had hit the fan,
From being like wasps around the jam,
They took off just like migrating birds,
Uttering no departing words.

I learnt what couldn't be taught in school,
A painful, but essential rule,
Trust too soon and your heart will sink,
For people aren't always what you think.

I naively thought they'd always be there,
But the raw truth was they didn't care,
Now left to drift on a lonely sea,
I've learnt just to rely on me.

I'm stronger now as each day ends,
Because I've left behind my so-called friends.

Freedom

Freedom is the sound of birds who sing at every dawn,
Freedom is the crying of a baby, newly born.
It is the thundering hooves of many horses running wild,
Its fate is held inside the heart and mind of every child.

Freedom is the new found smile upon the lips once more,
Of young and old whose country has been torn apart by war.
Freedom is to drive your car upon the open road,
Or it's the unburdening of a heavy mental load.

Freedom is an animal released out from its cage,
Or, it is two foes, who sign for peace upon the page.
Freedom is a country where two races don't collide,
But live their lives in harmony, together, side by side.

Freedom is a place in which you do not live in fear,
Or to scream and shout your loudest where nobody else can hear.
Freedom is a dolphin that does grace the ocean blue,
However large or minor, what does freedom mean to you?

The Wild West

It lay undiscovered many centuries ago,
A land dense with innumerable large buffalo.
With breathtaking prairies, and azure blue lakes,
Red dusty deserts, with cacti and snakes.

It personified freedom, it was untouched by fear,
When Christopher Columbus first landed here.
Such beauty, such vastness they thought was unknown,
But to the natives who lived there, this land was their home.

In the years that followed many battles were fought,
Between these foreigners, and the Indians whose land they sought.
It was clear a fresh era was starting to dawn,
And the country to be known as America was born.

Some talked of the freedom, others talked of their fear,
As they set out to conquer the Wild West frontier,
And when the war for independence was finally won,
The celebrations quickly begun.

There came many settlers from far away lands,
Their fleets of tall ships docked on crisp virgin sands.
A chance for a new life was what they'd been told,
Come see the New World, abandon the old.

Farmers imagined pastures so plush,
Others hoped to strike it rich in the latest gold rush,
The white-covered wagons of homesteaders' trains
Inspired generations to travel the plains.

Their hunger for freedom had outweighed the fear,
But no one imagined how tough it was here,
Death, starvation, diseases and pain
The struggle to outwit this hazardous terrain.

Many towns sprung up, as if overnight,
Their crude timber buildings became a regular sight,
They were lawless and dangerous and soon bore the scars,
Of drunken fights in seedy saloon bars.

Cowboys passed through on long cattle drives
Stealing hearts and taking lives.
There were outlaws and villains who went on the run,
And soon a man's best and only friend was his gun.

They didn't say things like 'freedom', they didn't use words like
    'fear',
If you're looking for justice you won't find it here.
Recognised by the shiny badges they wore,
Sheriffs were appointed to uphold the law.

Soon the railroad progressed at a rate so immense,
Cross-country it went at the natives' expense.
In the name of peace many treaties were signed,
But most were broken somewhere down the line.

A proud Indian warrior plots the fate of his race,
With bright feathered headdress and war-painted face,
He thinks, 'Maybe one day when this hatred's no more,
We'll ride the great plains like we did once before.

We once knew of our freedom, now we just live in fear,
But we'll fight till the bitter end we know is so near,
They've taken our culture, our homes and our land,
And our only revenge was at Custer's last stand.

The buffalo they slaughtered, killed by the ton,
For a hoard that seemed limitless, now there's virtually none.
On reservations reluctantly placed,
An uncertain future is what we all faced.
In our grandchildren's lifetime we pray that there'll be,
A day when the great native spirit's set free.

Perhaps then we'll know freedom in a world without fear,
Will our visions all come into being one year?
Until then we'll do what we can to survive
We'll dance day and night till there's no one alive.'

But shortly the frontier breathed its last,
And the legends into the wilderness passed.
Of all the names there were to symbolise the West
There were some that came to be known the best.

Many today are legends still, like Wyatt Earp and Buffalo Bill,
Annie Oakley and Billy the Kid, such stories were told of the
    things they did.
All the outlaws, villains, thieves and crooks
Can now only be seen in films and books.

The West still exists for the tourists to see,
Kept alive for the sake of this huge industry.
All the ranches, museums, the re-enactments of fights,
Are now part of a list of visitors' sights.

Now films charting freedom and stories of fear,
Are all that remain of the Wild West frontier.
So the West had been won, but at such a high cost,
For the dead and forgotten it was certainly lost.

Letter from Rangoon

'Dear Mother, I've put pen to paper tonight,
A full moon lets me read the words that I write,
I hope that you and Father are both keeping well,
I regret I have limited good news to tell.

This tropical climate's like nothing on earth,
The terrain here is sodden and has little worth,
The men are frustrated from shortage of sleep,
Our stomachs are hungry, our bodies are weak.

The rush when letters from back home arrive,
Keep our fading spirits alive.
I long for the day when this fighting will cease,
When I come home to England and re-live the peace.

To play cricket on Sundays for the village team;
Right now it all seems such a distant dream,
I'm afraid for now though, I must say goodbye,
Please try not to fret, or worry, or cry.

Take care and remember I'll see you all soon,
When I return back home from Rangoon.'

Nearly three days later, poised and armed,
There came the long awaited command,
And so he went in mortal defence,
Embarked in a battle newly commenced.

Where he crouched repeatedly firing his gun,
While his friends fell beside him, one by one,
Maimed to the extent that no one could tell,
Who once lived in this body, now a lifeless shell.

Onwards he waded through carnage and blood,
Soiling his boots in the sea of red mud,
Until finally luck abandoned his side,
And he too, collapsed in the chaos and died.

Sprawled face down in the swampy mire,
Distorted by brutal enemy fire,
No chance to surrender his final breath,
Conflict in life brought freedom in death.

Many decades later he's talked of as brave,
But the epitaph words simply read "No known grave",
For like countless comrades who wound up the same,
Little is left to show for his pain.

No dignified burial, no marble white cross,
All the letters he wrote home have since now been lost.
But as the seasons roll by now, year after year,
Preserved in evergreen youth, he lays here.

For like many before him who fell to their doom,
He never did come back from Rangoon.

A Tribute To Marilyn

Up in the sky a tiny star,
Seems so near, but yet so far;
Just like a child of tender years,
Filled with wishes, dreams and fears.

In life's book we write the page,
As we grow and learn with age,
No one knows or can predict
Who is chosen, who is picked.

For now and then a star is called,
To come and grace our earthly world,
The rules aren't easy in this game,
This fickle thing that's known as fame.

But one star made it all the way,
A high price she was made to pay,
For as if she'd waved a magic wand,
She became the world's most famous blonde.

Through her films she wowed the world,
Such beauty and glamour was unfurled,
But behind the camera, time and again,
She found it hard to hide the pain.

Anxious, lacking self-esteem,
Things weren't always what they seemed,
For as her fame just grew and grew,
She turned to drugs to help her through.

A lonely life right till the end,
It was diamonds that were her best friend,
And when so young she had to go,
We said farewell to Miss Monroe.

Now, years since she met her fate,
Many have tried to imitate,
But rival her no one could,
The greatest star from Hollywood.

Now even though she's long since gone,
Through her films she still lives on,
This legend of our movie screen,
We won't forget you, Norma Jean.

For your star still shines so bright,
And we're all dazzled by the light.

Why Can't I Cry?

The wells from which my tears once cried
Flowed on and on until they dried.
I wish my sea would wash ashore,
For maybe then I'll grieve some more.

I hear the droning sound of rain
As it pounds against my window pane,
I step outside, stare into space
And feel the droplets touch my face.

These artificial rivers flow,
They take my make-up as they go,
But hear me say, 'It's not my fault',
There is no trace of human salt.

So someone tell me, why, oh why,
Please tell me, just why can't I cry?
I have a heart, for I am whole,
I feel such pain as any soul.

So did my river lose its source?
Or take a more misleading course?
Perhaps that pond, with shimmering shine
Dried out and then slipped in decline.

Whatever it is has gone too far,
For empty is my reservoir.
Someday, it might be as before,
Or maybe I'll just cry no more.

The Other Side of Christmas

A child walks the street so sad and alone,
Two years ago he ran away from home,
With each step his miserable footsteps drag,
His world he keeps in one carrier bag.

He passes a window and pauses to look,
The scene inside could come straight from a book,
There's tinsel, tassels, turkey and such,
This feast for his eyes soon becomes all too much.

He stretches on tiptoe, nose pressed to the pane,
His eyes widen further then further again,
As he struggles to see all the countless delights,
It's so long since he saw more splendid a sight.

On the door is nailed a large holly wreath,
A tree in the corner has presents beneath,
There are streamers that glisten and baubles that shine,
On the fireplace are stockings, all hung in a line.

A log fire crackles and spits in the hearth,
While wine-sipping adults so heartily laugh,
Fun-loving children with smiles so wide,
Rattle their presents to guess what's inside.

Just then a young man comes into sight,
And puts down his wine glass on a shelf to his right,
He walks to the window and whilst giving a glare,
Draws the curtains with not a care.

The boy takes a step back, but he's starting to cry,
He wipes a single tear from his eye,
Then down the street he wanders away,
A shop doorway is where he'll spend his Christmas Day.

A Poem for the Bereaved

Where I have gone there is no pain,
No thunderclouds, no morning rain,
No murky black of winter skies,
No nasty thoughts, no wicked lies.

Where I have gone there is no greed,
No preference to age or creed,
No lifetime's winnings not been won,
No blinding light from angry sun.

Where I have gone there is no hate,
No reasons to intimidate,
No poverty, no class divide,
No laws to break or to abide.

Where I have gone I now am free
From all the ills that troubled me.
So remember this one saving grace;
Where I am now must surely be a better place.

For an Unborn Child

She's not yet a part of
This world so tossed and torn,
Let's change the world we live in
Before this child is born.

So she won't know of prejudice
For one of another race
But treat him as a brother
And turn to look him in the face.

So she won't know such violence,
Of murder, guns or rape,
Or live in a society
From which there's no escape.

It's up to us to bring the change,
Whatever it may take,
And make our world a safer place
For all our children's sake.

Rainbow's End

They say at the end of a rainbow,
You'll find a pot of gold,
But you either have to be lucky,
Or wise when you grow old.

But be warned; what some people lust after,
This shiny, metallic thing,
Can't guarantee the happiness
That simpler things may bring.

To me a person can be rich
In other ways besides
Having an abundance of money
And flaunting the status it provides.

For you can own the biggest house
And you can buy the newest car,
But when you need a shoulder to cry on,
Then it won't go far.

True wealth is found in a friend
Who'll be there through good times and bad,
Who'll share your joy and excitement,
And comfort you when you're sad.

To help achieve your goals
When you're feeling ten feet tall;
But if life doesn't go as you planned it,
They'll catch you when you fall.

If you've truly got a fortune,
It's not in silver or stone,
But a loving close-knit family,
In a comfortable happy home.

These are truly priceless,
More than any locket or charm,
They'll provide you with security
And protect you from any harm.

Life can be ever tricky,
And at the most trying of times,
Before you confront each hurdle,
You must first read the signs.

For money can buy material things,
Valued in pounds and pence,
But for health, love and happiness
The price is too immense.

So, you see, riches aren't just gems,
They can be found in the truest friend,
And I know what I'd rather discover
When I reach my rainbow's end.

Breathe Deep

"Breathe deep, my friend, breathe deep," he said,
To the man who lay dying, right there in his bed.
Droplets of sweat glistened on his forehead
As his blood pressure rose when his failing heart sped.

The assembly of loved ones, they started to weep
As the man settled back and fell into a sleep,
That pose now forever he's destined to keep,
Breathe deep, my friend, breathe deep.

Night-Time

The sun sets and loses its fiery glow,
Beyond the horizon it sinks so low,
To make way for the dusky shroud of night,
With a sky softly sprinkled with shimmering starlight.

We look up at the moon from here on the ground,
At something so natural, but perfectly round,
As it casts its shadow down on us all,
So near but so far, and deceptively small.

At just after midnight it's still shining strong,
And continues to do so all the night long,
Until it falls with the coming of dawn,
When yet another new day is born.

But outside my window it's the usual sight,
Only the flickering of an old street light,
The wind gently rustles the leaves on the trees,
They sway to and fro with the force of the breeze.

Then all becomes quiet, peaceful and still,
The wind gently dies down, as if at will,
Then through the dustbins a cat starts to creep,
But the rest of the world, it seems, is asleep.

The Old Photograph

An old picture frame, all dusty and worn,
Contains an old photograph, faded and torn.
In absence of colour, there's just dark and light,
Their faces stare back in plain black and white.

The expressions are harrowed, troubled and bleak,
Their willowy, slender bodies look weak.
Huddled together, they stand ever nearer,
Dressed in clothes from a bygone era.

Each with his own different story to tell,
Each with his own different version of hell.
Long were the days when the work was so tough,
Life for these working-class people was rough.

But this piece of history tells of our past,
Thanks to this picture's anonymous cast.
Although I'll never know what life was like then,
I'll look at this photo again and again.

And let my mind wander back all those years,
To think of the many hardships and tears
And think of the times when they managed to laugh,
And wonder who're the people in this old photograph.

The Soldier

The soldier who fought in a battle,
In the years thirty-nine, forty-five,
Will think not of what drove him to conflict
But give thanks he was one who survived.

Through days of gunfire and shelling,
The smell of death at its worst,
With a heavily laden kit-bag
And craving of hunger and thirst.

The soldier who thinks of a comrade,
With whom he fought alongside,
In years to come will grieve
Of how so early in life he died.

And now in a field filled with crosses
Is where these heroes unsung
Will sleep forever and ever
And remain eternally young.

But the soldier who thinks of a battle,
Which took place before he was born,
Will never know of such bloodshed,
Nor on such a large scale will he mourn.

Instead he can think of the courage
Of these men who stared death in the face
And those who met their fate
To make our world a better place.

We should all think of our freedom,
Compared to a war's living hell,
Where young men gave their lives
Just to be buried where they fell.

Future generations should learn
Of the sacrifice and sorrow
And remember those who gave up their today
For our tomorrow.

Forever

I'll love you forever, if forever is a night,
That slips into the morning when the dawn brings in its light,
A night compared in wonder to the turning of the tide,
Like the spell you put me under when I'm standing by your side.

I'll love you forever, like a crisp new morn in spring,
When the wind whispers its journey and the birds so softly sing.
When spiders' webs are glistening, with beads of sparkling dew,
I'll be forever listening for new words to say to you.

I'll love you forever, like a tree of evergreen,
That in the snow stands tall above where lesser plants have been.
And like the burning sun above, that melts the wicked frost,
Life won't disintegrate a love, never to be lost.

I'll love you forever, look no further than tomorrow,
I'll share your tears of happiness, I'll comfort you in sorrow.
Don't ask of me directions, down this rocky road of life,
There'll be time for reflections, when we live as man and wife.

I'll love you forever, and when on our wedding day,
The words "I do", I hope to hear you turn to me and say,
Then we'll start our lives as one, until the twelfth of never,
Come rain or thunder, snow or sun, I will love you forever.

The Florence Mary

In Southwold harbour, here to stay,
The *Florence Mary* sits today.
This senior citizen of boats
Upon the waves no longer floats.

Perhaps in many years gone by,
She sailed beneath a sapphire sky,
Admiring eyes were surely cast
When other vessels drifted past.

But, alas, it is no more,
For now she lives upon the shore;
A nautical retirement home,
Forgotten ships left all alone.

Now her remaining years will be
Spent beside the Southwold sea,
Where seagulls fly with not a care
And the smell of fish does fill the air.

Where visitors now all pass by,
No longer does she catch their eye,
For *Florence Mary* hasn't heard
That faster boats are now preferred.

So soon her paint is quick to fade,
Her final trip was long since made,
And as her wood begins to rot,
Sophisticated she is not.

But for me she holds a special charm,
As she sits beside the waters calm,
And I think she'll forever be
A grand old lady of the sea.

Grandfather

An elderly man with silver-tinged hair,
Sits all alone in a large armchair,
A chance to reflect on the many shed tears
In his life, cruelly swallowed by the passing years.

A few shiny medals nearby in a drawer
Are legacy to his role in a war.
Of death and destruction he had his fill
The memories of which do haunt him still.

For when he reached the golden sand
And descended upon this tropical land,
Did he ever imagine he would learn
That none of his friends would ever return?

To look into a dead man's eyes,
To hear the agonising cries,
Was someone dying? Who could tell?
What could prepare him for this hell?

Now years on he still sees this plight,
In fact he sees it every night,
He hears the sound of pain and fear
But they're screams no one else can hear.

But of so many he's just one
Who fought beneath this burning sun,
And of the dead let's not forget
That we remain to them in debt.

My heroes are grandfathers far and away,
Who made the world what it is today.
Remember the past and remember the truth
Because for our freedom they gave up their youth.

The White Wedding Gown

Tell me, do you remember when,
We were the talk of the town?
You in your black and grey top hat and tails
And me in my white wedding gown.

A posy of cream carnations I held,
They gave the sweetest smell,
And I recollect a single one
Pinned onto your lapel.

As I joined you at the altar, you turned
And softly spoke to me,
You said that I was the loveliest thing
That you did ever see.

We exchanged our vows, and then the rings,
And as the church bells pealed,
I knew that from that moment on
Our love was forever sealed.

Arm in arm we walked the aisle,
Then waiting just outside
A photographer snapped you and I
With joyous smiles so wide.

Twelve precious months I had with you
In which was born our son,
And such affection was bestowed
Upon this child so young.

But, contentment came to pass,
And happiness was no more,
For you were called away to fight
In a bitter, destructive war.

Reluctantly you said farewell,
Before you left my side,
And every night into my pillow
I so sadly cried.

For you broke my heart in two,
Never to be healed,
When I learnt you'd lost your life
Upon some Flanders field.

To die so young, so far away
It was an awful waste,
For our son would grow
To not recall his father's face.

But of his mother he is fond,
For she taught him to be strong,
And to prepare him for his adulthood
She told him right and wrong.

To make her happy once again,
When he was fully grown,
He married a lovely girl
And raised a family of his own.

But soon his mother left this world,
Her spirit flew up above,
To be this time forever more
With her first and only love.

Gone, but not forgotten,
For as the generations unfold,
The story of their tragic love
Is so often told.

And now in a house, on a modern estate,
Upon the edge of a town,
Hangs that picture of him, in his top hat and tails,
And her in her white wedding gown.

ME
(Myalgic Encephalomyelitis)

Why do I feel like this tonight?
I've lost all hope and will to fight,
Please help me try and understand,
God, is this all part of your plan?
You let me shout, you let me cry,
Yet give me no excuses why,
Such hostile feelings, coiled and pent,
I know I need to let them vent,
Inside, my body's tossed and torn,
My face is pale and so forlorn,
It hides frustration, fear and pain,
Am I really ill, or just insane?
People smile and shake my hand,
Yet they don't really understand,
Inside I want to make amends,
To strangers who were once my friends.
Without them I have learned to cope,
With feelings of eluding hope,
Now developing inside of me,
An inner strength to set me free.
One day I know there'll come a time,
When I alone will truly shine,
Patiently I'll wait my turn,
And let the world just watch and learn.

Then everyone who left my side,
Will see the turning of the tide,
A different me will be unveiled,
And then we'll really see who's failed,
Rewarding those who gave their love.
One day I'll truly rise above;
Until that day I'll have to wait,
And see what's chosen as my fate,
I won't give in, I'll stand and fight,
Not let the dark eclipse the light.
I feel I'm at the moment wrapped,
In something in which I'm firmly trapped,
I'm lost – please find me
And break these chains that bind me.

Goodbye

Don't weep for me when I am dead,
Some words are better left unsaid,
I'll live on in your heart and mind,
And in memories of the nicer kind.

Don't pity me when I am gone,
For when I bid this world 'so long',
Away so far will fly my soul,
In the search to find another role.

Don't cry, or say that life's unfair,
For it won't be me who's lying there,
My spirit will be upward bound,
Before my bones are underground.

So on the evening of my death,
When I submit my final breath,
Look up into the twinkling light,
For there'll be an extra star that night.